Kids Writing Practice Workbook

Jewish History in America
Practice writing sentences.

I0458537

By: Ellie Tiemann

Learn about 24 Jewish Americans from US History.

Contact the author :
aworldoflanguagelearners@gmail.com

In this workbook you will learn about the contributions of Jewish Americans in US History from the 1600s until present day. On the first page of each person, you will read facts about each person. Then there is space for you to write sentences about that person. After you write about the person go back and use the sentence writing checklist to make sure that you have written you best sentences. Then on the next page write about the same person using your best handwriting.

Asser Levy	Bilhah Abigail Levy Franks	Haym Salomon	Judah Touro	Rebecca Gratz	Penina Moïse
Levi Strauss	Emma Lazarus	Hinda Amchanitzky	Hannah G. Solomon	Lillian Wald	Albert Einstein
Rose Schneiderman	Ray Frank	Beatrice Alexander	Bob Marshall	Ezra Jack Keats	Bella Abzug
Ruth Bader Ginsburg	Jeffrey Hoffman	Robert Lawrence Stine (R.L. Stein)	Sally Priesand	Debbie Friedman	Sharon Kleinbaum

Jewish Americans to Read and Write About

Asser Levy born before 1651 -1680

Bilhah Abigail Levy Franks 1688–1746

Haym Salomon 1740-1785

Judah Touro 1775 - 1854

Rebecca Gratz 1781–1869

Penina Moïse 1797- 1880

Levi Strauss 1829-1902

Emma Lazarus 1849-1887

Hinda Amchanitzky 1850-1910

Hannah Greenebaum Solomon 1858-1942

Lillian Wald 1867-1940

Albert Einstein 1879-1955

Rose Schneiderman 1882-1972

Ray Frank 1861-1948

Beatrice Alexander 1895-1990

Bob Marshall 1901-1939

Ezra Jack Keats 1916-1983

Bella Abzug 1920-1998

Ruth Bader Ginsburg 1933-2020

Jeffrey Hoffman 1944-current

Robert Lawrence Stine (R. L. Stine) 1943-current

Sally Priesand 1946-current

Debbie Friedman 1951-2011

Sharon Kleinbaum 1959-current

Sentence Writing

- Start each sentence with a capital letter.
- A sentence has a subject. This is who or what the sentence is about.
- A sentence has an action, it is also called the predicate. This tells what is happening in the sentence.
- Check your sentences for correct spelling.
- A sentence needs punctuation marks. A sentence ends with either a period, question mark, or explanation mark.

.	?	!

subject   action

Capital letter   Punctuation

Pronouns

A pronoun takes the place of a noun.

Singular			Singular Possessive	
	I	me		my	mine
	you	you		your	yours
masculine	he	him	masculine	his	his
feminine	she	her	feminine	her	hers
gender neutral	they	them	gender neutral	their	theirs
object	it	it	object	its	its

Asser Levy

📖 **Read the facts.**

Pronouns: he/him

was born before 1651

died in 1682

left Europe for religious freedom

was the first Jewish butcher in New Amsterdam

was first Jewish citizen in New Amsterdam

✏️ **Write about the person using complete sentences.**

_____

_____

_____

_____

_____

_____

Sentence Writing Checklist

Capital letter	Has a subject	Has an action	Spelling	Punctuation
☐	☐	☐	☐	☐

Asser Levy

_____

_____

_____

_____

_____

_____

_____

_____

Bilham Abigail Levy Franks

📖 **Read the facts.**

Pronouns: she/her

was born in 1688

died in 1749

kept kosher

wrote letters to her son

had her portrait painted

✏️ **Write about the person using complete sentences.**

_____

_____

_____

_____

_____

_____

Sentence Writing Checklist

Capital letter	Has a subject	Has an action	Spelling	Punctuation
☐	☐	☐	☐	☐

Bilham Abigail Levy Franks

_____

_____

_____

_____

_____

_____

_____

_____

Haym Salomon

📖 **Read the facts.**

Pronouns: he/him

was born in 1740

died in 1785

immigrated to New York

started a business

loaned his money to the fight for American independence

Write about the person using complete sentences.

_____

_____

_____

_____

_____

_____

Sentence Writing Checklist

Capital letter	Has a subject	Has an action	Spelling	Punctuation
☐	☐	☐	☐	☐

Haym Salomon

_____

_____

_____

_____

_____

_____

_____

_____

_____

Judah Touro

📖 **Read the facts.**

Pronouns: he/him

was born in 1775

died in 1854

was a merchant

fought in the war of 1812

donated money to libraries and Jewish organizations

✎ **Write about the person using complete sentences.**

_____

_____

_____

_____

_____

_____

Sentence Writing Checklist

Capital letter	Has a subject	Has an action	Spelling	Punctuation
☐	☐	☐	☐	☐

Judah Touro

_____

_____

_____

_____

_____

_____

_____

_____

_____

Rebecca Gratz

📖 **Read the facts.**

Pronouns: she/her

was born in 1781

died in 1869

donated to charities

started religious school for Jewish children

starred a Jewish foster home

✏️ **Write about the person using complete sentences.**

_____

_____

_____

_____

_____

_____

Sentence Writing Checklist

Capital letter	Has a subject	Has an action	Spelling	Punctuation
☐	☐	☐	☐	☐

Rebecca Gratz

_____

_____

_____

_____

_____

_____

_____

_____

_____

Penina Moïse

📖 **Read the facts.**

Pronouns: she/her

was born in 1797

died in 1880

published the first poetry book as a Jewish American women

wrote songs for her congregation

was a teacher

✏️ **Write about the person using complete sentences.**

_____

_____

_____

_____

_____

_____

Sentence Writing Checklist

Capital letter	Has a subject	Has an action	Spelling	Punctuation
☐	☐	☐	☐	☐

Penina Moïse

Levi Strauss

📖 **Read the facts.**

Pronouns: he/him

was born in 1829

died in 1902

ran a dry goods business

started a company that sold blue jeans

donated money to charities

✏️ **Write about the person using complete sentences.**

_____

_____

_____

_____

_____

_____

Sentence Writing Checklist

Capital letter	Has a subject	Has an action	Spelling	Punctuation
☐	☐	☐	☐	☐

Levi Strauss

_____

_____

_____

_____

_____

_____

_____

_____

_____

Emma Lazarus

📖 **Read the facts.**

Pronouns: she/her

was born in 1775

died in 1854

published poems

advocated for Jewish refugees

wrote the lines used on the Statue of Liberty

✎ **Write about the person using complete sentences.**

_____

_____

_____

_____

_____

_____

Sentence Writing Checklist

Capital letter	Has a subject	Has an action	Spelling	Punctuation
☐	☐	☐	☐	☐

Emma Lazarus

_____

_____

_____

_____

_____

_____

_____

_____

_____

Hinda Amchanitzky

📖 **Read the facts.**

Pronouns: she/her

was born in 1850

died in 1910

immigrated to the US

opened restaurants

published the first Yiddish cookbook in the US

Write about the person using complete sentences.

_____

_____

_____

_____

_____

_____

Sentence Writing Checklist

Capital letter	Has a subject	Has an action	Spelling	Punctuation
☐	☐	☐	☐	☐

Hinda Amchanitzky

_____

_____

_____

_____

_____

_____

_____

_____

_____

Hannah Greenebaum

📖 **Read the facts.**

Pronouns: she/her

was born in 1859

died in 1942

advocated for woman suffrage

founded the National Council

aided immigrants

✏️ **Write about the person using complete sentences.**

_____

_____

_____

_____

_____

_____

Sentence Writing Checklist

Capital letter	Has a subject	Has an action	Spelling	Punctuation
☐	☐	☐	☐	☐

Hannah Greenebaum

_____

_____

_____

_____

_____

_____

_____

_____

Lillian Wald

📖 **Read the facts.**

Pronouns: she/her

was born in 1867

died in 1940

fought for public health care

advocated for women's rights

ran the Henry Street Settlement

✍ **Write about the person using complete sentences.**

_____

_____

_____

_____

_____

_____

Sentence Writing Checklist

Capital letter	Has a subject	Has an action	Spelling	Punctuation
☐	☐	☐	☐	☐

Lillian Wald

_____

_____

_____

_____

_____

_____

_____

_____

_____

Albert Einstein

📖 **Read the facts.**

Pronouns: he/him

was born in 1879

died in 1955

was a theoretical physicist

earned the Nobel Prize in physics

immigrated to the US

✏️ **Write about the person using complete sentences.**

_____

_____

_____

_____

_____

_____

Sentence Writing Checklist

Capital letter	Has a subject	Has an action	Spelling	Punctuation
☐	☐	☐	☐	☐

Albert Einstein

_____

_____

_____

_____

_____

_____

_____

_____

_____

Rose Schneiderman

📖 **Read the facts.**

Pronouns: she/her

was born in 1882

died in 1972

was the first woman elected to a national labor union

worked towards equal pay for woman workers

helped Jewish refugees

Write about the person using complete sentences.

_____

_____

_____

_____

_____

_____

Sentence Writing Checklist

Capital letter	Has a subject	Has an action	Spelling	Punctuation
☐	☐	☐	☐	☐

Rose Schneiderman

_____

_____

_____

_____

_____

_____

_____

_____

_____

Ray Frank

📖 **Read the facts.**

Pronouns: she/her

was born in 1861

died in 1948

was a religious-school teacher

was the first Jewish woman to preach formally from a pulpit

stopped working when she got married

✎ **Write about the person using complete sentences.**

_____

_____

_____

_____

_____

_____

Sentence Writing Checklist

Capital letter	Has a subject	Has an action	Spelling	Punctuation
☐	☐	☐	☐	☐

Ray Frank

_____

_____

_____

_____

_____

_____

_____

_____

_____

Beatrice Alexander

📖 **Read the facts.**

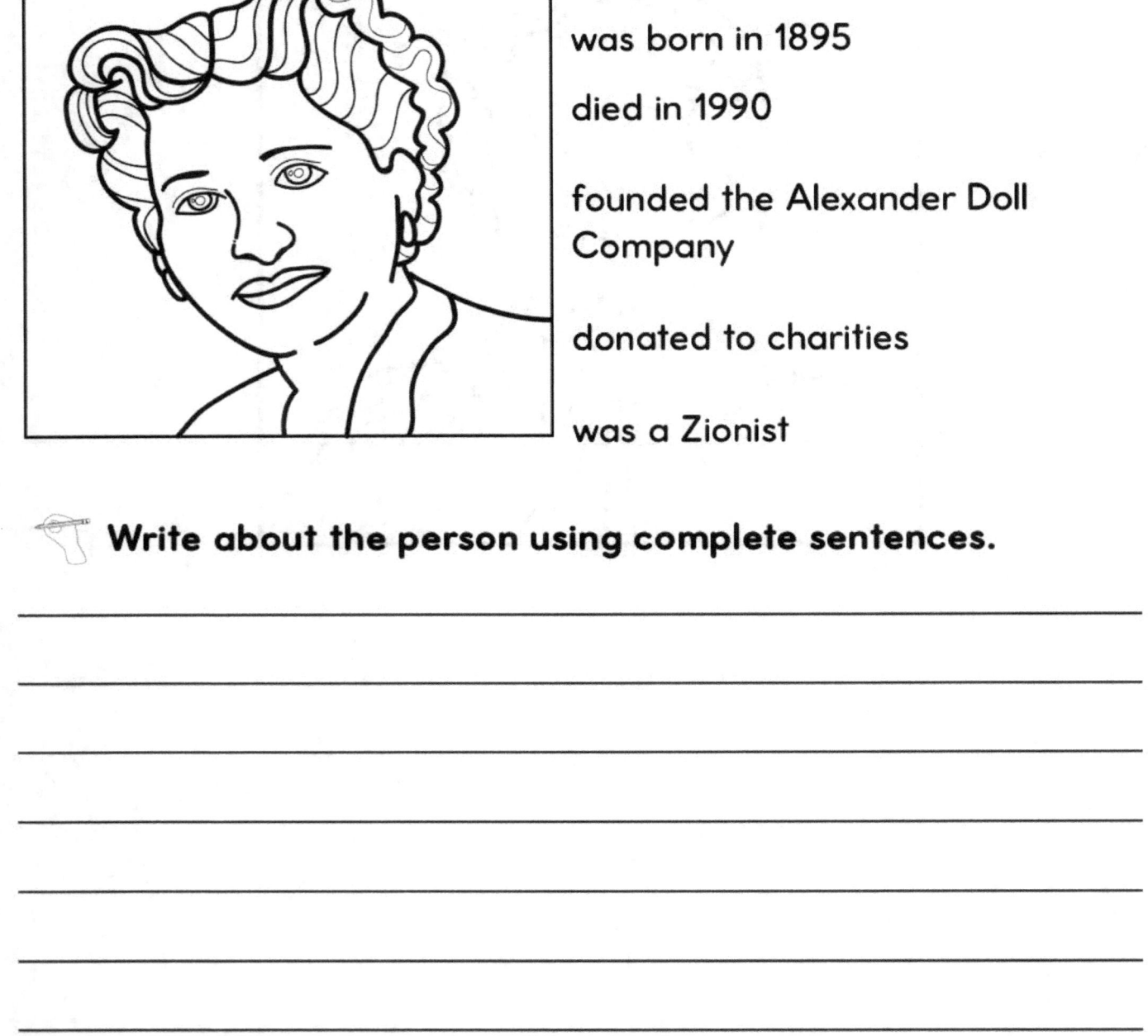

Pronouns: she/her

was born in 1895

died in 1990

founded the Alexander Doll Company

donated to charities

was a Zionist

Write about the person using complete sentences.

_____

_____

_____

_____

_____

_____

Sentence Writing Checklist

Capital letter	Has a subject	Has an action	Spelling	Punctuation
☐	☐	☐	☐	☐

Beatrice Alexander

_____

_____

_____

_____

_____

_____

_____

_____

Bob Marshall

📖 **Read the facts.**

Pronouns: he/him

was born in 1901

died in 1939

earned a PhD in forestry

worked to preserve the Arctic National Wildlife Refuge

founded the Wilderness Society

✏️ **Write about the person using complete sentences.**

_____

_____

_____

_____

_____

_____

Sentence Writing Checklist

Capital letter	Has a subject	Has an action	Spelling	Punctuation
☐	☐	☐	☐	☐

Bob Marshall

_____

_____

_____

_____

_____

_____

_____

_____

_____

Ezra Jack Keats

📖 **Read the facts.**

Pronouns: he/him

was born in 1916

died in 1983

was an children's book author

was an illustrator

won the Caldecott Medal

✏️ **Write about the person using complete sentences.**

_____

_____

_____

_____

_____

_____

Sentence Writing Checklist

Capital letter	Has a subject	Has an action	Spelling	Punctuation
☐	☐	☐	☐	☐

Ezra Jack Keats

_____

_____

_____

_____

_____

_____

_____

_____

_____

Bella Abzug

📖 **Read the facts.**

Pronouns: she/her

was born in 1920

died in 1998

was a lawyer

worked against the House Un-American Activities Committee

helped start the nationwide Women Strike For Peace

Write about the person using complete sentences.

_____

_____

_____

_____

_____

_____

Sentence Writing Checklist

Capital letter	Has a subject	Has an action	Spelling	Punctuation
☐	☐	☐	☐	☐

Bella Abzug

_____
_____
_____
_____
_____
_____
_____
_____
_____

Ruth Bader Ginsburg

📖 **Read the facts.**

Pronouns: she/her

was born in 1933

died in 2020

was a mother

was the first woman to receive tenure at Columbia Law School

was the first Jewish woman to serve on the Supreme Court

✏️ **Write about the person using complete sentences.**

_____

_____

_____

_____

_____

_____

Sentence Writing Checklist

Capital letter	Has a subject	Has an action	Spelling	Punctuation
☐	☐	☐	☐	☐

Ruth Bader Ginsburg

_____

_____

_____

_____

_____

_____

_____

_____

_____

Jeffrey Hoffman

📖 **Read the facts.**

Pronouns: he/him

was born in 1944

is still alive

is an astrophysicist

was NASA's first Jewish male astronaut

has flown to space 5 times

Write about the person using complete sentences.

_____

_____

_____

_____

_____

_____

_____

Sentence Writing Checklist

Capital letter	Has a subject	Has an action	Spelling	Punctuation
☐	☐	☐	☐	☐

Jeffrey Hoffman

_____

_____

_____

_____

_____

_____

_____

_____

_____

Robert Lawrence Stine (R.L. Stine)

📖 **Read the facts.**

Pronouns: he/him

was born in 1943

is still alive

writes scary books

is a father

produced movies

🔫 **Write about the person using complete sentences.**

_____

_____

_____

_____

_____

_____

Sentence Writing Checklist

Capital letter	Has a subject	Has an action	Spelling	Punctuation
☐	☐	☐	☐	☐

Robert Lawrence Stine (R.L. Stine)

_____

_____

_____

_____

_____

_____

_____

_____

_____

Sally Priesand

📖 **Read the facts.**

Pronouns: she/her

was born in 1946

is still alive

was the first women ordained as a rabbi

was a painter

was a pulpit rabbi

✏️ **Write about the person using complete sentences.**

_____

_____

_____

_____

_____

_____

Sentence Writing Checklist

Capital letter	Has a subject	Has an action	Spelling	Punctuation
☐	☐	☐	☐	☐

Sally Priesand

_____

_____

_____

_____

_____

_____

_____

_____

_____

_____

Debbie Friedman

📖 **Read the facts.**

Pronouns: she/her

was born in 1951

died in 2011

wrote songs

sang songs

created accessible Jewish music

✎ **Write about the person using complete sentences.**

_____

_____

_____

_____

_____

_____

Sentence Writing Checklist

Capital letter	Has a subject	Has an action	Spelling	Punctuation
☐	☐	☐	☐	☐

Debbie Friedman

_____
_____
_____
_____
_____
_____
_____
_____
_____
_____
_____

Sharon Kleinbaum

📖 **Read the facts.**

Pronouns: she/her

was born in 1959

is still alive

is a Reconstructionist rabbi

advocates for gays and lesbians, immigrants, Palestinians, women, and people of color

is a mother

✏️ **Write about the person using complete sentences.**

_____

_____

_____

_____

_____

_____

Sentence Writing Checklist

Capital letter	Has a subject	Has an action	Spelling	Punctuation
☐	☐	☐	☐	☐

Sharon Kleinbaum

_____

_____

_____

_____

_____

_____

_____

_____

_____

Terms of Use

Thank you for purchasing this product.
The contents are the property of Ellie Tiemann and licensed to you only for classroom/personal use as a single user. I retain the copyright, and reserve all rights to this product.

You may not claim this work as your own, giveaway, or sell any portion of this product. You may not share this product anywhere on the internet or on school share sites.

Find more teaching resources at

https://www.teacherspayteachers.com/Store/A-World-Of-Language-Learners

Get weekly tips and find out about teaching resources at

https://www.aworldoflanguagelearners.com/newsletter/

www.ingramcontent.com/pod-product-compliance
Lightning Source LLC
Chambersburg PA
CBHW081725120626
46550CB00010B/3258